DEREK JETER
#2

DEREK JETER #2

THANKS FOR THE MEMORIES

DAVID FISCHER

SPORTS PUBLISHING

To my captain, Carolyn, with love.

Contents

Introduction

As we look back at Derek Jeter's career and try to capture its many memorable moments and achievements in one volume, we've got good news and bad news. The good news is that so many memories have been created, so many records smashed, so many unforgettable victories won that it's difficult to whittle it down to so few pages.

This book will trace Jeter's legendary baseball career, from his early minor league struggles, to his exhilarating days as a Yankee superstar, to his status as an enduring symbol of the steroid-free athlete. Indeed, his intangible ability to play at a high level in the postseason makes him the face of the modern Yankees dynasty—and of America's national pastime.

Fans of Jeter have witnessed events that are carved indelibly into the collective memory of baseball, like his unforgettable dive into the stands, his dramatic 3,000th hit, his November home run, the Flip Play, his farewell speeches at the old Yankee Stadium and to "The Boss," George Steinbrenner.

All the sights and sounds you associate with Jeter are here, too. The sly, dimpled smile, those famous green eyes. Chanting Jeter's first and last names—*Der-ek Jee-tah! Der-ek Jee-tah!*—with thousands of other raucous fans. All those wonderful interactions with youngsters while waiting for his turn at bat, that inside-out swing producing a line-drive single to right field so unlike anything that had come before (and few have come since), the rhythmic clapping of hands after rounding first base. The softly sonorous, oh-so-familiar voice of Bob Sheppard—"Now batting for the Yankees . . . number 2 . . . Derek Jeter . . . short-stop . . . number 2."

All that, my friends, is more than you could fit in a hundred scrapbooks.

You'll relive your own memories of Jeter's career as you page through this book—your first game watching him play at Yankee Stadium, the view of him leading the team out of the dugout and onto the field to start the game . . . the time you got his autograph . . . the afternoon you saw him collect four hits.

Derek Jeter's sensational career is a baseball story for the ages: a skinny, biracial kid from Michigan who grew up to become New York's most beloved sports figure. Of course you know the bad news is that the 2014 season is Jeter's final season wearing pinstripes. So as we close the book on his brilliant career, you can be sure that Jeter's march toward the Hall of Fame has been dignified and certain; he exemplifies leadership and displays a hero's grace. Now that Jeter is hanging up his spikes, his jersey #2 will be retired by the world's most famous sports franchise. He walks in the footsteps of Ruth, Gehrig, DiMaggio, and Mantle, and someday his shadow will loom just as large.

DEREK JETER
#2

Inning One

THE KID FROM KALAMAZOO

A biracial kid from Michigan grows up to be drafted by the only team he ever wanted to play for. But Derek struggles in the minor leagues, when homesickness and poor performance on the field threaten to end his career.

"My upbringing was like *The Cosby Show*. We had fun, always did a lot of things together. My parents were involved in every-thing my sister and I did."
—Derek Jeter

Derek with his family at a ceremony hon-oring his 3,000th career hit. From left to right with Derek are his younger sister Sharlee, his mother Dorothy, and his father Dr. Charles Jeter.

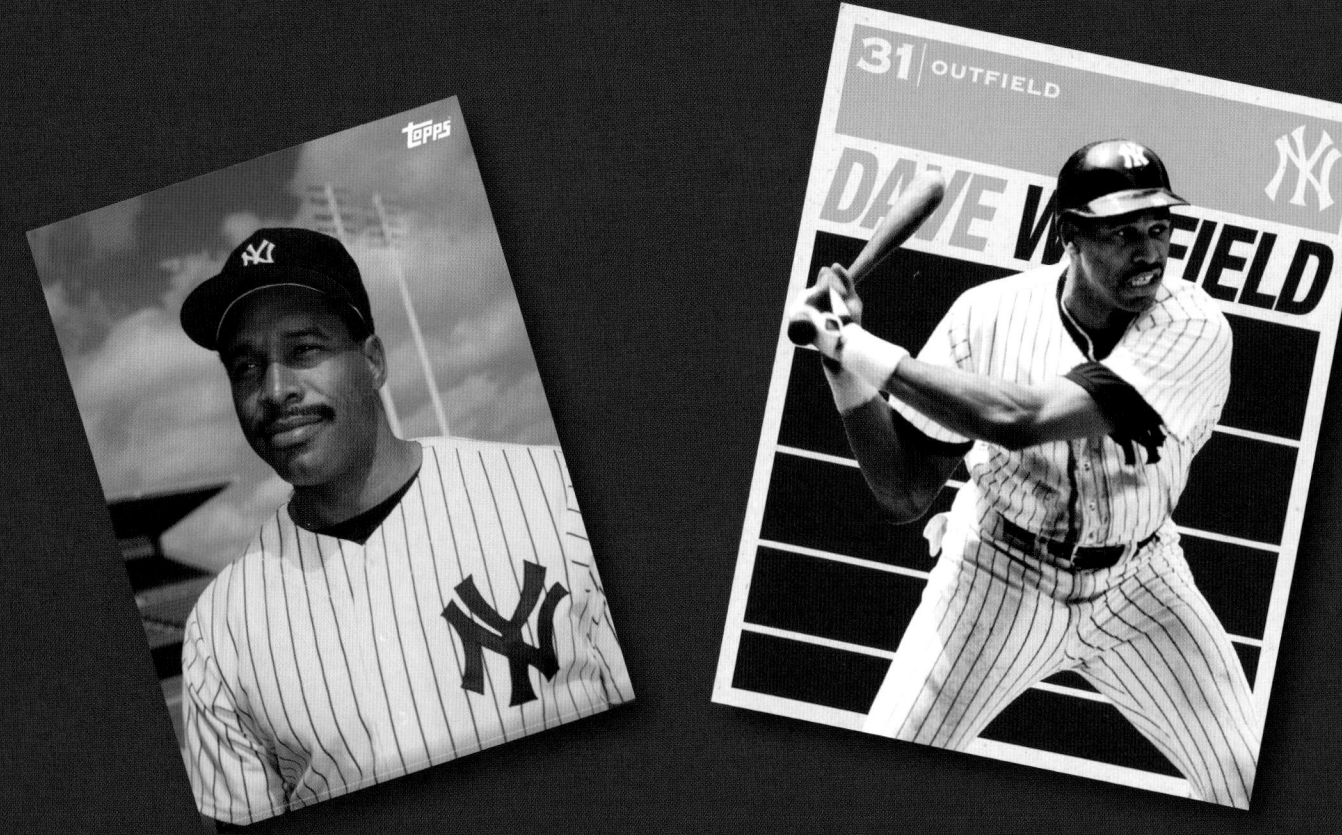

"All I ever wanted to be was a Yankee. When I was a kid I was always hoping there'd be a jersey left for me to wear with a single digit."
—Derek Jeter

Derek was born in New Jersey but raised in Kalamazoo, Michigan, where a poster of Dave Winfield hung on his bedroom wall. He grows up wanting to be the shortstop for the New York Yankees, and his wish comes true.

Derek at Kalamazoo Central High School in 1992. After an impressive high school career, including a .509 batting average his senior year, Derek wins several national sports awards, including being named the 1992 Gatorade High School Athlete of the Year and *USA Today*'s High School Player of the Year.

"He's more than just a baseball player. He's Derek."
—Dorothy Jeter

COLORADO ROCKIES FREE AGENT REPORT

Adjusted OFP	61		CO ID No.		
Basic OFP	54		Report No.	1	
Cross-check			Position	SS	
PLAYER	JETER (Last Name) DEREK (First Name) S (Middle Name)		ST	MICH.	
School/Team	CENTRAL H.S.	City KALAMAZOO	HT 603 WT 180 Bats R	Throws R	
CLASS: (HS.) JC. SO. JR. (SR)	DOB 06-26-74	KALAMAZOO (City)	MICH. (ST)	49007 (Zip)	

Current Address ___
Current Telephone ___ City KALAMAZOO ST ___ Zip ___
Permanent Address SAME
Permanent Telephone SAME

Scout SANTA, E.

Date 05-08-92 Games 3 Innings 14

RATING KEY

80 — Outstanding
70 — Very Good
60 — Above Average
50 — Average
40 — Below Average
30 — Well Below Average
20 — Poor

Use One Grade
Grade On Major
League Standards
Not Amateur

NON-PITCHERS	Pres.	Fut.
Hitting Ability		
Power	20	40
Running Speed	20	40
Base Running	60	60
Arm Strength	50	60
Arm Accuracy	60	70
Fielding	60	60
Range	50	60
Baseball Instinct	50	60
Aggressiveness	50	60
	50	50

Pull ___ Str. Away ___ Opp. Field ___
X
60 - UPPER DECK
Raw Pwr ___

PITCHERS	Pres.	Fut.
Fast Ball		
FB Movement		
Curve		
Control		
Change of Pace		
Slider		
Other		
Poise		
Baseball Instinct		
Aggressiveness		
Arm Action		
Delivery		
Type		

MAKE-UP

Desire/Drive	EXCEL
Emotional Control	GOOD
Hustle/Intensity	EXCEL
Intestinal Fortitude	GOOD
Mental Toughness	GOOD
Self Confidence	GOOD
Work Habits	GOOD

Previously Drafted ___
Club(s) ___
Round(s) ___
Date Eligible 06-92

Agility: V. GOOD Phys. Maturity: FAIR Glasses: NO

Physical Description
PERFECT SS BODY. VERY PROJECTIBLE. LOOSE AND ATH. LONG LEGS W/ STRNGTH. LONG LOOSE ARMS. POT TO GET STRNGER IN UPPER BODY. REMINDS ME OF GARY GREEN - REDS.

Abilities
EXCEL LOOSE ARM + THROWING MOTION. ACTIVE LWR BODY. HANDS WORK WELL. GOOD RANGE. RUNS EASY. HAS NATURAL FLOWING MOVEMENTS. O.K. APP TO HITTING W/ SOME BAT SPEED

Weaknesses
OCC STRAIGHTENS FRONT ARM + SWEEPS BAT. FIELDS BALL OFF RIGHT SIDE. ATH ENUF TO ADAPT + IMPROVE.

Summation and Signability Group: I THIS GUY IS SPECIAL. YOU GET EXCITED JUST WATCHING HIM WARM UP. ALL-STAR POT AS SS AT ML LEVEL. RAISED OFP 7 PTS: ABILITY TO PLAY PREMIUM POS AT ML LEVEL. SIGNED W/ MICHIGAN AS A SECURITY BLANKET. WILL SIGN.

Colorado Rockies scout Ed Santa gives Derek rave reviews in this free-agent report from May 8, 1992: "This guy is special. You get excited just watching him warm up. All-Star potential as SS at ML level." The Rockies hold the 27th overall selection in the draft, so they never have a shot at Derek. The Yankees grab him with the sixth pick.

Derek on a 1992 Topps trading card, the year he is selected by the Yankees with the sixth pick in the amateur draft.

Two months after graduating high school, Derek, age eighteen, visits Yankee Stadium and joins catcher Jim Leyritz, center, and infielder Mike Gallego in a pre-game workout on September 12, 1992. Playing rookie ball in Tampa that summer, Derek batted only .210 and struck out 52 times in 58 games. He had never before spent a night away from home without his family and later admitted, "I cried every night. It was the first time in playing baseball that I struggled."

Self-doubt affected his fielding, too. In 1993, Jeter was promoted to the Class A Greensboro Hornets and he ended up in the record books for a most ignominious reason—his 56 errors in 126 games were the most committed in one season by any player in South Atlantic League history.

Derek attends his first major league training camp in the spring of 1994 and by October is on the cover of *Yankees Magazine* as the face of the team's future.

"I was only there [at spring training] two weeks, but I got an opportunity to see these players. And that's when I said to myself, 'It's not that they're throwing 100 miles an hour faster, or hitting 400 feet longer. They're just doing things more consistently.' And then I thought, 'Well, I can do some of those things. Not as consistently, but I'm capable of doing it.' That was the defining moment that helped turn my career around."

—Derek Jeter

The top prospect receives *Baseball America*'s Minor League Player of the Year trophy at Yankee Stadium on September 14, 1994.

By 1995, Derek was playing full time with the Triple-A Columbus Clippers. Here he demonstrates the early Jeterian swing.

Derek warms up prior to making his major league debut at the Kingdome in Seattle on May 29, 1995. The scrawny, twenty-one-year-old rookie whiffs once and goes hitless in five at bats against the Mariners. The next day he records his first major league hit off pitcher Tim Belcher and comes around to score his first run on Jim Leyritz's double.

"He had alert eyes. He took in what was going on around him and made adjustments. He wanted to fit in. You could see his skill set was going to allow him to be pretty good."
—Buck Showalter

Derek's career starts inauspiciously with an 0-for-5 night in his first major league game on May 29, 1995. "I'll just try to go out and have fun. And try to improve," Jeter said after an 8–7 loss to the Mariners.

The improvement began the next evening when he collects his first big league hit off Seattle's Tim Belcher, a fifth inning single. The hit came in front of a Kingdome crowd of fewer than 11,000 fans, none of whom knew they were witnessing history.

"He got the ball, but it wasn't a lot of pomp and circumstance on his side," said manager Buck Showalter. "It was, 'Well, that's my job—to get a hit. When do I get my next opportunity to get another one?'"

Jeter finished the game going 2-for-3 with two runs scored in a 7–3 Yankees loss.

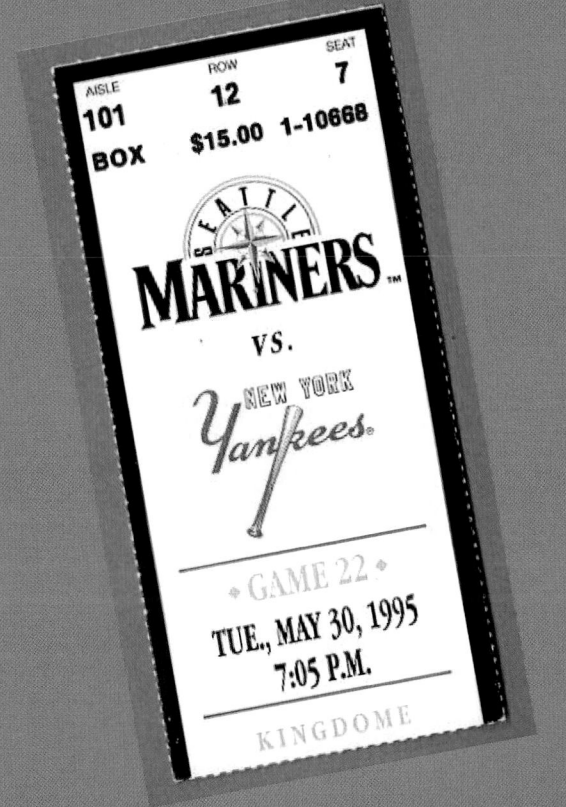

Ticket stub to the game of Derek's first major league hit.

Inning Two

ROOKIE OF THE YEAR

In his first season, Jeter leads the Yankees to the franchise's first World Series title in eighteen years.

Derek displays his athleticism jumping over J. T. Snow while completing a double play against the Angels on May 27, 1996. A new dynasty begins this season thanks to the spark of the rookie shortstop.

"I'm trying to think who the best Yankee shortstop I've ever seen is, and I keep coming back to this kid."
—Phil Rizzuto

Derek is the first Yankees rookie to start at shortstop on Opening Day in thirty-four years. He hit .314 this season and emerged as a team leader with maturity far beyond his twenty-two years. Now a perennial all-star, Derek is one of those rare players to have spent his entire career with one team.

The Yankees were trailing the Orioles 4–3 in Game 1 of the 1996 American League Championship Series. In the bottom of the 8th inning, Derek hit a fly ball to the right-field wall that Baltimore's Tony Tarasco seemed about to catch, but twelve-year-old fan Jeffrey Maier reached over with his mitt and deflected the ball. It was ruled a home run, and the Yankees went on to win the game, the series, and the world title.

Derek tags out Marquis Grissom trying to steal second base in the fifth inning of the decisive Game 6 of the 1996 World Series. The Yankees defeated the Atlanta Braves for their first title since 1978. Overall, Derek batted .361 in the postseason, helping to lead the Yankees back to prominence.

SEC
U24
TIER RESERVE

BOX/ROW
C

SEAT
10
$45.00

WORLD SERIES

1996

WORLD SERIES
World Series®

WHAT A GAME!™

Yankees®

GAME 6

VS

NATIONAL LEAGUE CHAMPIONS

Yankee Stadium

RAIN CHECK
Rain Check subject to the conditions
set forth on back hereof.
DO NOT DETACH THIS COUPON.
Office of the Commissioner

GAME 6

This 1996 World Series ticket got a lucky fan into the clinching Game 6 at Yankee Stadium.

Inning Three

CHAMPIONSHIP METTLE

After the Yankees win the 1996 World Series, Derek leads the team to three more championships in the next four years. He is never considered the best player in baseball—he isn't even considered the best player on his team. But his ability to play big in the clutch is legendary.

Derek launches a home run against the Seattle Mariners on August 29, 1998. This is a magical season for Derek and the Yankees. The team wins a record 125 games including the postseason (against just 50 losses), and Derek finishes with a .324 batting average and a league-leading 127 runs scored.

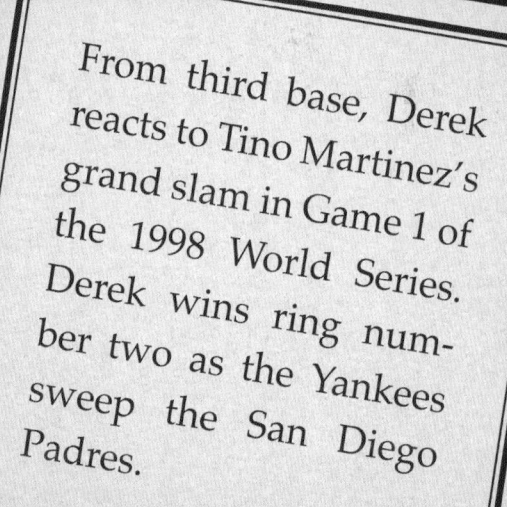

From third base, Derek reacts to Tino Martinez's grand slam in Game 1 of the 1998 World Series. Derek wins ring number two as the Yankees sweep the San Diego Padres.

Derek scores the go-ahead run in the Game 4 clincher of the 1998 World Series as the Yankees win their 24th World Championship. Derek has a terrific series, batting .353 in the four games, with six hits, four runs scored, and one run batted in. The team's ultimate achievement caps a season of personal milestones for "Jeets," which include the first of 13 All-Star selections and the first of eight 200-hit seasons.

"I want to thank the Good Lord for making me a Yankee"
—Joe DiMaggio

Derek and the Yankees make it look easy in Game 4 of the 1999 World Series, completing back-to-back series sweeps and extending the Yankees' World Series-winning streak to twelve consecutive games. Derek goes 6-for-17 against Atlanta's talented pitching staff and bats .375 for the entire postseason.

Derek in the tunnel leading to the locker room after the Yankees play baseball's last game of the century and complete a four-game World Series sweep of the Atlanta Braves on October 27, 1999. This sign is the one artifact Derek asks for from the original Yankee Stadium.

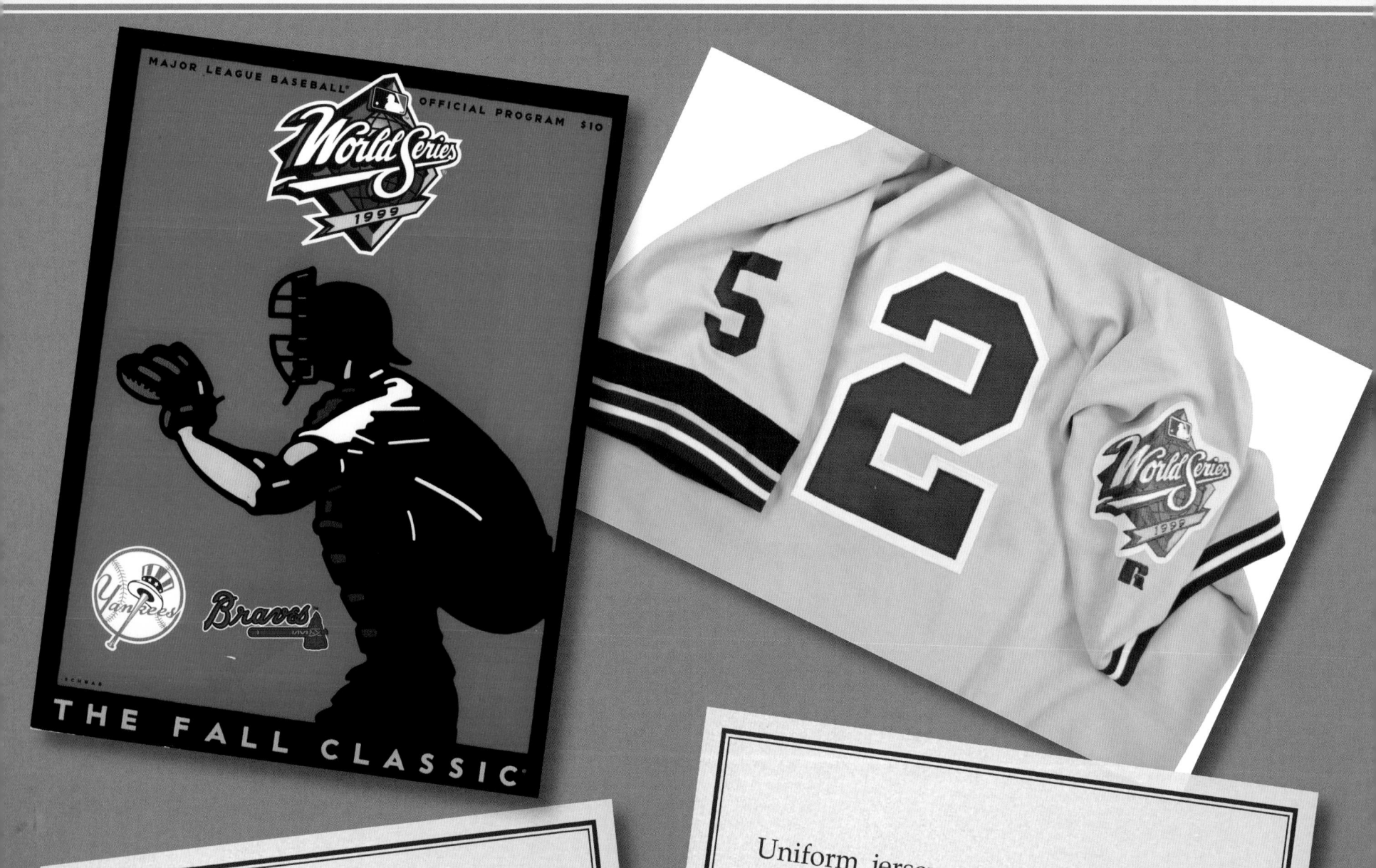

1999 World Series Official Program

Uniform jersey worn by Derek in the 1999 World Series. Joe DiMaggio (#5) had died earlier that season.

"He's a credit to his team and the city."
—Mike Piazza

Derek eludes the tag of Mets catcher Mike Piazza to score the tying run in Game 3 of the 2000 World Series at Shea Stadium. The Mets went on to win the game 4–2, snapping the Yankees' streak at 14 straight wins in the World Series.

Straphangers used these New York City subway tokens to get from Yankee Stadium in the Bronx to Shea Stadium in Queens. The 2000 World Series was New York's first Subway Series in forty-four years.

Derek leads off Game 4 of the 2000 World Series by blasting Bobby Jones's first pitch into the left-field seats, making manager Joe Torre look like a genius for moving Jeter into the leadoff spot in the batting order. Derek's blast sets the tone for the Yankees, turning back any momentum the Mets had after winning Game 3.

Derek hits .409 against the Mets (9-for-22) with two doubles, a triple, and two home runs. The twenty-six-year-old continues his staggering success in the postseason, especially on the biggest stage, extending his World Series hitting streak to 14 games.

After beating the Mets in the 2000 World Series, Derek is indicating four championships in five years, and it's his third straight Series crown.

"It has been an incredible honor having a front row seat for one of the great players of all time. Derek has been a winner every step of the way."
—Brian Cashman

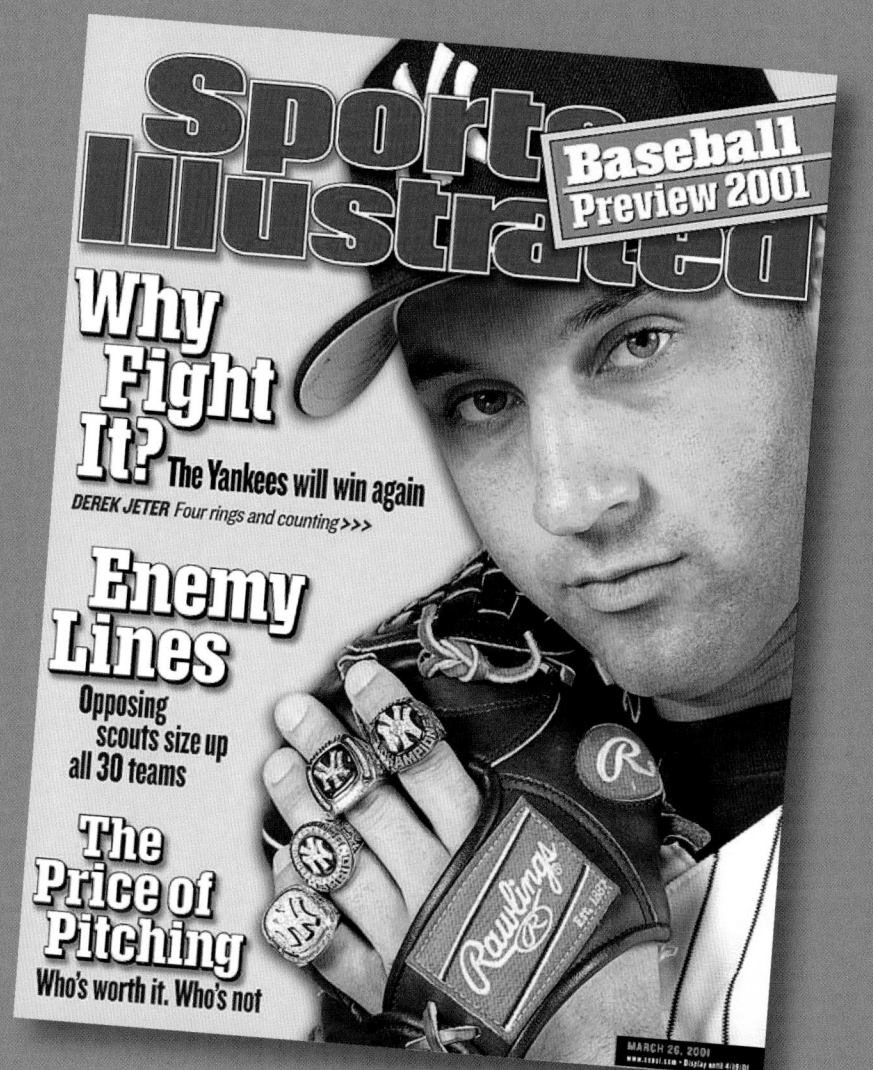

Derek, showing off his jewelry collection on the cover of the 2001 *Sports Illustrated* Baseball Preview Issue, will wait eight years for a fifth ring.

Inning Four

FACE OF A DYNASTY

Derek becomes the prince of the city and squires some of the world's most beautiful women. Yet he remains a private person, considerate to his fans and respected by teammates and opponents alike.

"Derek Jeter is the kind of player who one day I will get to say, 'I played with him.'"
—Paul O'Neill

"Until you hit 1.000 and make no errors, you always have something to improve on."
—Derek Jeter

Derek's signature jump throw. During the 1999 season he becomes a household name, leading the league in hits with a career-high 219 and achieving personal bests with 24 homers, 102 runs batted in, and a .349 batting average.

"[He's] the most recognizable athlete that we have in sports today. Just having the honor to suit up and play on the same field with him was amazing."
—Nick Swisher

On the field, Derek plays in superstar fashion. Off the field, he garners attention for his quiet confidence and good looks. He begins appearing in numerous commercials and is a much sought-after product pitchman.

Derek is on the town with actress Jordana Brewster in 2002. When you're the handsomely paid face of the sport's most famous franchise and play in the media capital of the world, you'll do well with the ladies. Derek has also been linked to Mariah Carey, Tyra Banks, Vanessa Minnillo, Jessica Alba, Scarlett Johannson, Adriana Lima, Jessica Biel, Minka Kelly, and Hannah Davis.

Derek appears on the cover of GQ magazine's April 2011 issue. "Don't get me wrong, it's not like I didn't go out and have fun," Jeter tells GQ. "But there's been a lot of players that come to New York and get caught up in the lifestyle, and before you know it, they're sent away to another team because it affected their performance. My number one priority was on the field. I've had fun. It's not like I've never gone out; I've done a lot of things. But I've always kept sight of my number one priority."

"He's legit. He's versatile; you see him on the cover of *GQ*, then the next week he's on the cover of *Sports Illustrated*. He's focused; he works hard. He's in a major market with a lot of pressure, but he handles the pressure. I'm proud of him."
—Michael Jordan

Derek is the cover boy of the April 2011 issue of *GQ*, magazine; three months later he will be voted America's favorite male athlete, according to a Harris Poll.

"He's very loyal. He's the kind of guy you'd want to raise your kids to be like or you want your daughter to marry. He's just a stand-up guy with a great deal of character. Unfortunately, there aren't a whole lot of those people around anymore."
—Joe Torre

Derek has earned the respect of coaches and peers, and the admiration of fans.

Derek uses his celebrity to help kids. In 2009 he is named winner of the Roberto Clemente Award for his charitable work with his Turn 2 Foundation. The foundation promotes a healthy lifestyle, academic achievement, and abstinence from drugs and alcohol. Since 1996, Turn 2 has awarded more than $19 million in grants to deserving kids.

"On and off the field, he's the way you want your kids to grow up. Only Jesus is perfect, but he's pretty close to that guy."
—Albert Pujols

"Derek . . . said when he got to the big leagues he wanted to start a foundation, and he did that in 1996. We started it back then when we didn't even know how long he'd be in the league. It was just a thing to give back to the community. I'm very proud of him. . . . This is a great award and it shows he's been recognized for something he feels is important."
—Dr. Charles Jeter

The Roberto Clemente Award is given annually to a player who demonstrates the values Clemente displayed in his commitment to community and understanding the value of helping others. Each club nominates a player in September. The winner is selected from thirty nominees during the World Series.

Derek is the third Yankee player to win the award, and the first in nearly twenty-five years. The other Yankee winners were Ron Guidry in 1984 and Don Baylor in 1985.

"It's nice to get an opportunity to focus on something that really has to do with something more than baseball. It has to do with community work and giving back to the community. I think people in our position should take advantage of it. . . . I know I'm being awarded for this right now, but there's a lot of players that give back to the community, and I think everyone should be commended for that."
—Derek Jeter

Derek playfully pulls Brian Roberts' jersey at Camden Yards in 2007.

"I think it was maybe 2004; I was on second or something and he just said, 'You can hit .300 in this league.' To hear it from someone like that, it just kind of opens your eyes. I don't think it's just me, I think he does it to everybody. But for some reason when he tells it to you, you think you're the most important person in the world. He's just kind of got that personality, and he's so good with people. . . . He's just always been that guy that encouraged me from the other side. I played against him obviously a ton. One of those guys that early in my career really actually helped me believe that I could play here at this level and play well."

—Brian Roberts

"Derek has been the benchmark for character and class in a baseball uniform. He has inspired a generation to play baseball the way it was meant to be played. It has been an honor to play against him."
—Evan Longoria

"You gotta have fun. Regardless of how you look at it, we're playing a game. It's a business, it's our job, but I don't think you can do well unless you're having fun."
—Derek Jeter

"When he spoke, people listened."
—Johnny Damon

"He made me a better player and a better person. I'm so proud of our friendship and I love him like a brother. Derek was a true champion and the greatest teammate I ever had."
—Jorge Posada

The glare never bothers Derek. No superstar athlete is more accessible; he is available by his locker before and after every game.

Inning Five

THE LEGEND GROWS

Despite the Yankees' failure to bring another World Series trophy to New York from 2001 to 2008, Derek's unrivaled reputation as a fearless leader is cemented by his knack for being in the right place at the right time, and for his intangible ability to make the big play on the biggest stage.

"The Flip" by Derek in Game 3 of the 2001 American League Division Series is one of the greatest improvisational plays in the history of baseball.

The Flip Play

The Yankees entered the 2001 postseason as the three-time defending champion and heavy favorite in the American League Division Series against the Oakland Athletics. But the Yankees got off to a rough start, losing the first two games of this best-of-five series in the Bronx. The dynasty looked dead as the Yankees traveled to Oakland with history against them. No team had ever won a best-of-five series after losing the first two games at home. Now the series had moved to Oakland and the Yankees were in danger of being swept. In the 7th inning of the third game, New York was clinging to a 1–0 lead. In the 7th with two outs, Oakland's Jeremy Giambi singled and Terrence Long doubled to the right-field corner. As the ball rattled off the wall, Giambi ran around third base heading for home. Right fielder Shane Spencer retrieved the ball and his throw toward the infield sailed over the cutoff man. Improbably, Jeter ran toward the first base line, grabbed the errant throw and made a backhand flip of the ball to catcher Jorge Posada, who tagged Giambi just before he touched the plate. The Yankees won the game and the series.

"It was like Superman flying out of the sky to save the season," said general manager Brian Cashman. The Yankees became the first team to lose the first two games of a best-of-five at home and then win the series. Derek delivered big. He batted .444 in the series and saved the Yankees from near-certain elimination with his hustle and instincts in Game 3. Nobody knows why Derek was in the right place at the right time. "It was my job to read the play," he said.

Derek's most famous highlight reel: his sprint across the field and backhanded flip relay to Jorge Posada, nailing Jeremy Giambi at home trying to score from first on a double. For some reason, Giambi did not slide. "If he slides," Posada said, "I don't have a chance."

"[The Flip] was no sultanic swat, no stopwatch sprint, no acrobatic catch. It was a simple sideways toss, of no more than 30 feet, physically unremarkable, except: Who else would be so intuitive? . . . Who else would be so in touch with those mystical messages that are transmitted to born winners?"

—Jonathan Lehman, *The New Republic*

Derek exults after the Yanks defeat the Seattle Mariners to clinch the 2001 American League pennant, earning him a fourth straight World Series appearance, and fifth in his six seasons in the major leagues.

Mr. November

Derek connects against Arizona's Byung-Hyun Kim and hits the winning home run in the 10th inning of Game 4 of the 2001 World Series, evening the Series at two games apiece on October 31. The home run stroke flashes just after the clock strikes midnight for the first ever November home run. Thus, Mr. November is born.

Derek trots around the bases, his right fist raised in the air, before jumping onto home plate and into the waiting arms of his jubilant teammates (right). The gravity of the moment is not lost on Derek. "I've never hit a walk-off homer," said the Yankees' new Mr. November. "I don't think I hit one in Little League. That was huge."

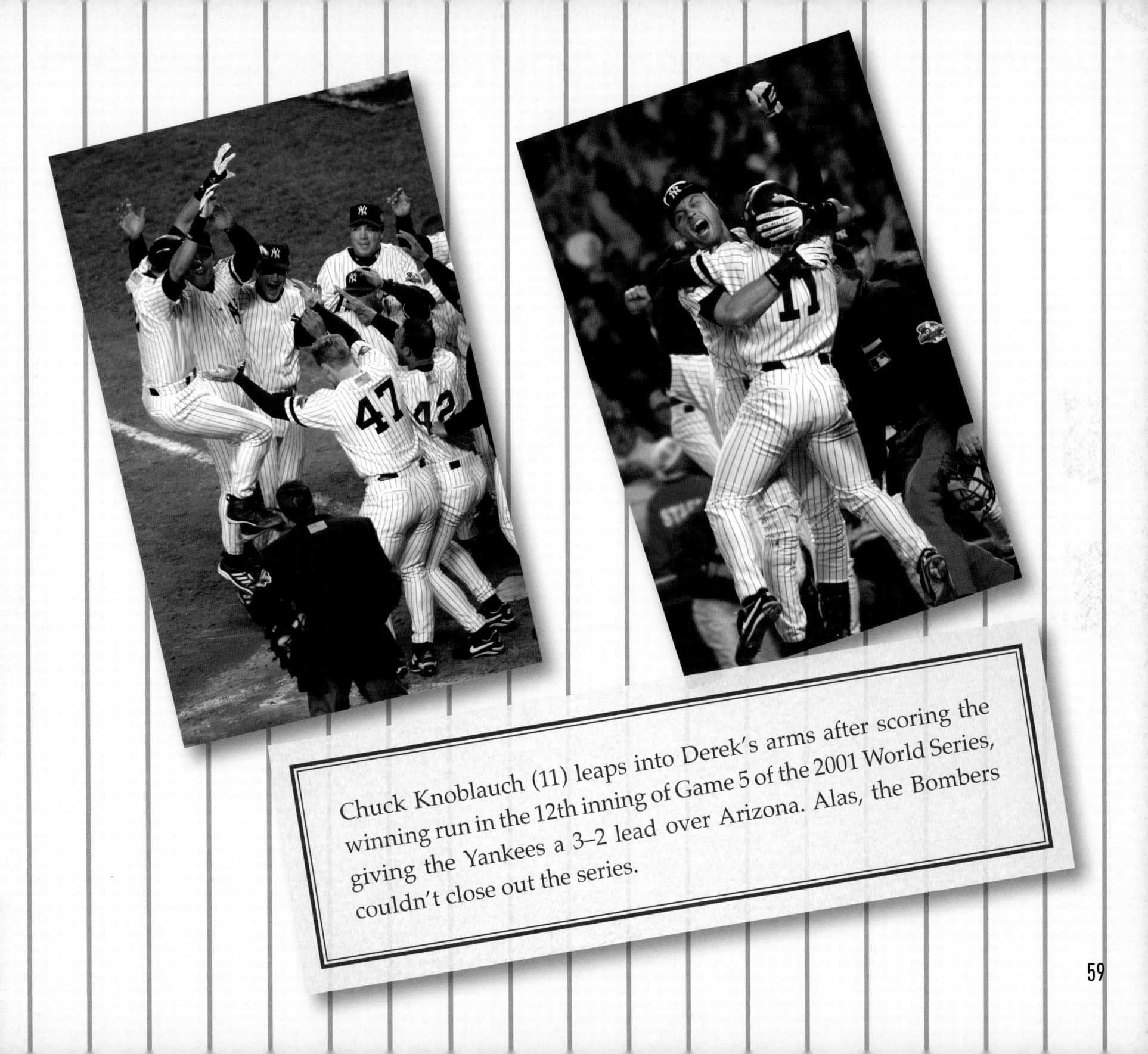

Chuck Knoblauch (11) leaps into Derek's arms after scoring the winning run in the 12th inning of Game 5 of the 2001 World Series, giving the Yankees a 3–2 lead over Arizona. Alas, the Bombers couldn't close out the series.

Taking Boston Red Sox pitcher Pedro Martinez deep in Game 3 of the 2003 American League Championship Series at Fenway Park. In Game 7, Derek sparks the game-tying rally against Martinez, setting up Aaron Boone's dramatic home run to send the Yankees to a sixth World Series appearance in eight years.

"I don't know if I believe in curses, or jinxes, or anything like that. But I'll tell you what I do believe—I believe in ghosts. And we've got some ghosts in this stadium."
—Derek Jeter

Derek has earned a reputation as a clutch player who has made some of the most famous plays in recent memory. When the Yankees need a big defensive play, there is Derek to sacrifice life and limb by diving into the stands face-first, emerging with a bloody chin, to make an incredible catch of a foul pop-up to save two runs in the top of the 12th inning against the Boston Red Sox, the team's most fierce rival, during the heated pennant race of 2004.

"He's what every player strives to be like. The career he's had speaks for itself. You grow up as a kid, he was the guy that was the face of baseball. He was in the playoffs every year, he's in the right place at the right time every play. If you're a baseball fan, regardless of who you cheer for, you respect the guy. He's what baseball's about."

—Brian McCann

"You can *hear* him running to first base every time."
—former Blue Jays manager Buck Martinez

The Yankees clinch another A.L. East division title in 2005, this time on the last weekend of the season at Boston's Fenway Park. Though Derek will bat .333 during the division series, the Yankees lose to the Angels in five games.

Derek's 2006 Upper Deck baseball card. He finishes the season second in batting average (.343) and runs scored (118) and third in hits (214). He wins the first of his five Silver Sluggers, awarded to the best offensive shortstop in the league.

Derek, the Yankees' Captain Clutch, has made a career of rising to meet the moment. In Game 1 of the 2006 division series he tops himself, going 5 for 5 and capping his night with a home run. He bats .500 in the series, but the Tigers win.

Inning Six

THE CANYON OF HEROES

Derek serves as spokesman for the closing of Yankee Stadium and the opening of the new Stadium, and then he guides the Yankees to their 27th World Series championship at thirty-five, an age when most shortstops have retired. His fifth victory parade is the sweetest.

Of Yankee uniform numbers 1 through 10, only #2 (Derek's) has not been retired—but it undoubtedly will be.

The 79th All-Star Game is played at Yankee Stadium on July 15, 2008. Forty-nine Hall of Famers take part in pre-game ceremonies, including Hall of Fame shortstops (from left to right), Ozzie Smith, Robin Yount, Ernie Banks, and Cal Ripken Jr. Derek will soon have his own bronze plaque in Cooperstown.

"Derek Jeter? Probably the best clutch player ever. Offensively, his accomplishments speak for themselves. Three thousand hits, more than 200 home runs, and a great batting average. . . . I'll put it this way: Of all the shortstops in history, he's the one I want out there in Game 7 of the World Series."

—Cal Ripken Jr.

Spikes worn by Derek in the last game played at the old Yankee Stadium.

"One of my biggest memories of Jeter was in 2008, that last year in the old Yankee Stadium. His speech to all the fans, that was classic. I was there, and I appreciate what he did for us, because no one else could have done it better than him."
—José Molina

Derek salutes fans after a stirring speech in the last game ever played at old Yankee Stadium.

He said: "From all of us up here, it's a huge honor to put this uniform on every day and come out here and play. Every member of this organization, past and present, has been calling this place home for eighty-five years. There's a lot of tradition, a lot of history, and a lot of memories. The great thing about memories is you're able to pass them along from generation to generation. Although things are going to change next year and we're going to move across the street, there are a few things with the New York Yankees that never change. That's pride, tradition, and, most of all, we have the greatest fans in the world. We're relying on you to take the memories from this stadium and add them to the new memories we make at the new Yankee Stadium, and continue to pass them on from generation to generation. We just want to take this moment to salute you, the greatest fans in the world."

Bat used by Derek in the final game played at the old Yankee Stadium.

Derek plays long toss at the new Stadium.

"Obviously, [Derek's] a student of the game. Obviously, he's kind of the field general out there on the field, and as a quarterback I have great respect for that. He's been doing it so well for so long."
—Peyton Manning

In 2009, Derek helps lead the Yankees to their 27th World Series title, the fifth for the shortstop since he broke into the majors in 1996. Derek bats .407 (11-for-27) in the World Series, and .344 for the entire postseason.

The 2009 New York Yankees Postseason Media Guide.

"All along, since I saw him for the first time, I knew that Derek was special. You knew you had something special with him."
—Mariano Rivera

Derek and Mariano Rivera admiring the World Series trophy after Mo secured the final out of the deciding Game 6 in 2009 against the Philadelphia Phillies at Yankee Stadium.

Derek celebrates his fifth World Series championship at the ticker tape parade along Broadway in 2009.

"You are Major League Baseball's foremost champion and ambassador. You embody all the best of Major League Baseball. You have represented the sport magnificently throughout your Hall of Fame career. On and off the field, you are a man of great integrity, and you have my admiration."
—Commissioner Bud Selig, in a letter to Derek Jeter after the 2009 season

"On those [championship teams from the 90s], those guys were young. . . . They had different roles. Derek Jeter wasn't a leader back then. Jorge Posada wasn't a leader then. They were the guys looking to the David Cones, the Paul O'Neills, . . . the veterans around them. But now this is those guys' team. They've taken over that leadership role. And they've proved they can deliver a championship with a whole new cast."
—Brian Cashman, after the Yankees won the 2009 World Series

One for the thumb: Derek's 2009 World Series ring.

Inning Seven

MR. 3,000

Jeter becomes the all-time Yankees hits leader and reaches the 3,000 hits milestone, a feat no Yankee had ever touched. He is among the all-time franchise leaders in several categories, and he is the most productive major league hitter in postseason history.

On July 9, 2011, Derek reaches 3,000 career hits in the most thrilling way possible—by hitting a home run! But he doesn't stop there, finishing with a perfect 5-for-5, including the go-ahead RBI in a 5–4 win.

"For those who say today's game can't produce legendary players, I have two words: Derek Jeter. As historic and significant as becoming the Yankees' all-time hits leader is, the accomplishment is all the more impressive because Derek is one of the finest young men playing the game today."
—George Steinbrenner

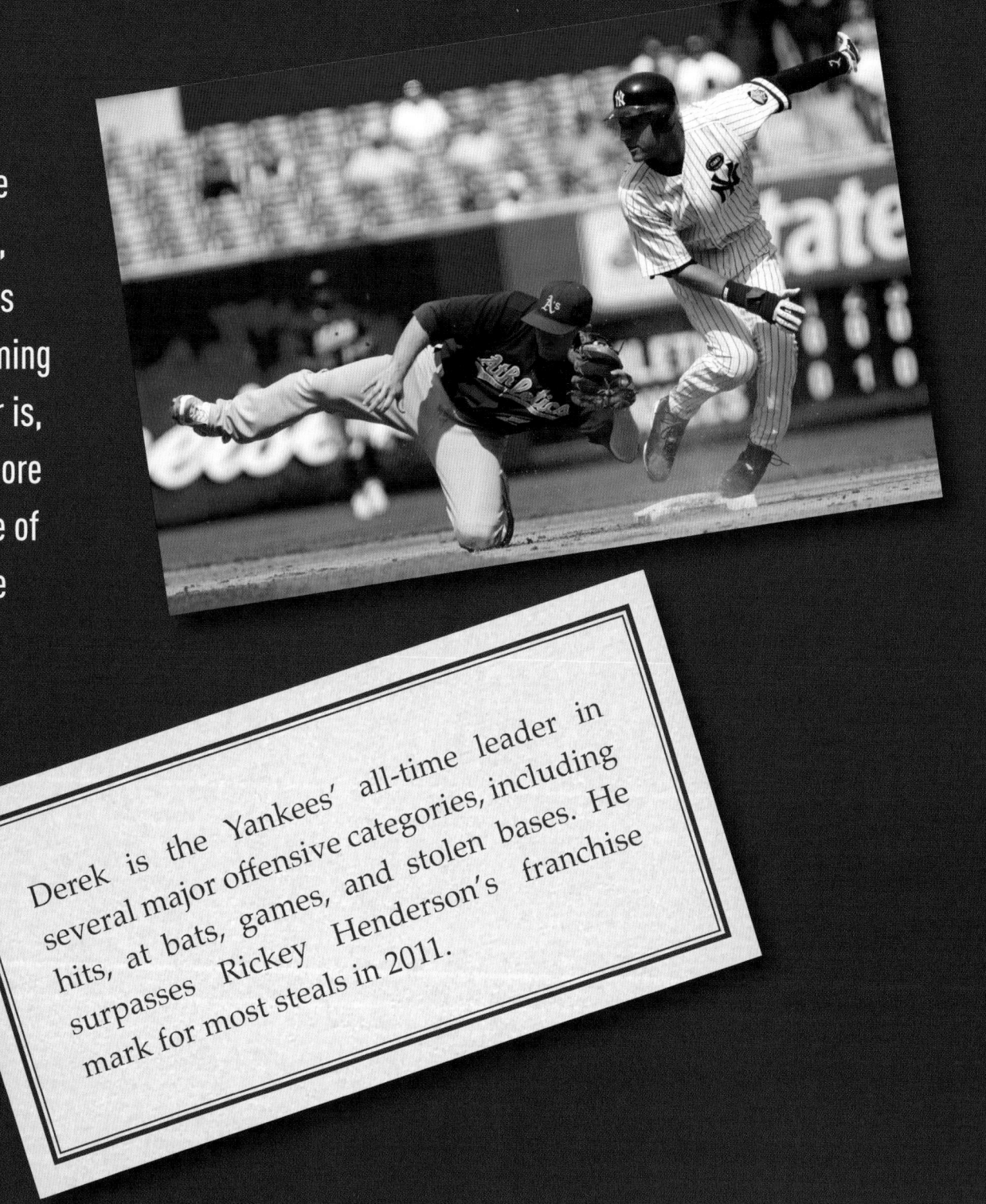

Derek is the Yankees' all-time leader in several major offensive categories, including hits, at bats, games, and stolen bases. He surpasses Rickey Henderson's franchise mark for most steals in 2011.

Derek salutes the home crowd after he becomes the Yankees' all-time hits leader when he picks up his 2,722nd career hit, passing legendary Hall of Famer Lou Gehrig's seventy-two-year-old mark on September 11, 2009.

"I think the way he's gone about his business, with consistency and just as a professional, being just stubborn enough to be great. He's been a joy to watch. He's everybody's favorite player."
—Reggie Jackson

"I never imagined, I never dreamt of this. Your dream was always to play for the team. Once you get here, you just want to stay and try to be consistent. So this really wasn't a part of it. The whole experience [was] overwhelming."
—Derek Jeter

Lineup card on the night Derek passes the Iron Horse and becomes the Yankees all-time leader in hits, with 2,722 hits.

"That combination of character and athletic ability is something he shares with the previous record holder, Lou Gehrig."
—George Steinbrenner

3,000 Hits

It was magical that on his second hit of the day, in his second at bat, Derek—#2—reaches the historic 3,000-hits milestone at 2:00 p.m. He is just the second player to do so with a home run (seen here connecting against Tampa Bay Rays lefthander David Price), and it was Jeter's first homer at Yankee Stadium in nearly a year.

"Happy to be part of history with a player [and] person of his caliber."
—David Price

Tampa Bay's Casey Kotchman, left, tips his cap to the 28th player to reach 3,000 career hits, and the only one of the Yankees' many greats to break the 3,000-hit barrier as a member of the team. Said Derek: "The thing that means the most to me is that I've been able to get all these hits in a Yankee uniform. No one's been able to do that before, which is hard to believe. I've grown up with these fans. They've seen me since I've been 20 years old."

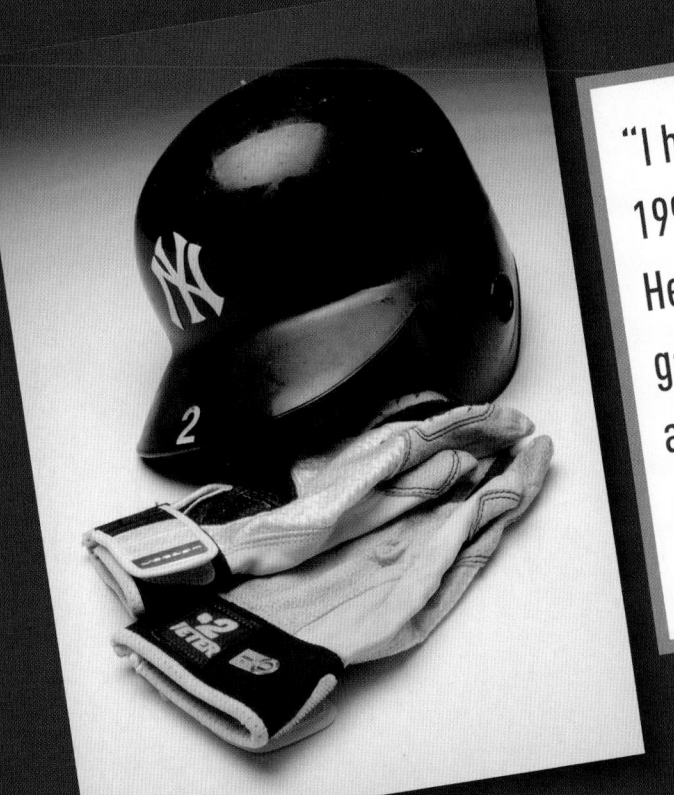

"I had the opportunity to play with Derek when he was a rookie in 1996, and I had no doubts that Derek would reach that milestone. He is a very consistent player and he never deviated from his game. When you stay healthy and you are consistent and compile a lengthy career like Derek has done, you have the opportunity to reach that 3,000-hit plateau."

—Wade Boggs, the first player to reach 3,000 hits with a home run

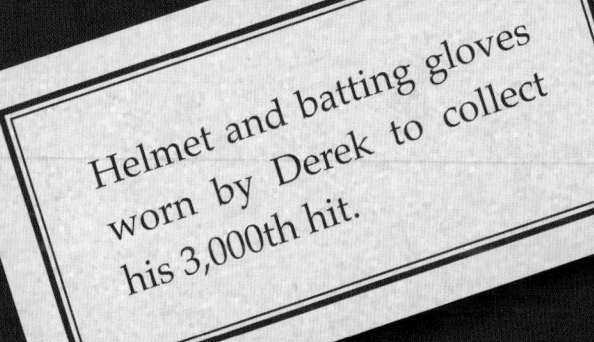

Helmet and batting gloves worn by Derek to collect his 3,000th hit.

"After 2,999, his next at bat the dugout was full. All our support staff, everyone . . . it was packed. You knew that something special was about to happen. It was kind of the scene when we had two outs in (Game 6 of) the World Series in 2009. It was packed."

—Joe Girardi

> "Three thousand hits is pretty good. But I think Jeter cares more about winning than the other stuff."
> —Yogi Berra

3,000 Hits With One Team

Jeter became the 28th member of the 3,000 hit club, but only the 11th club member to record all of their hits with one team. The others are: Cap Anson (Chicago Cubs), Craig Biggio (Houston Astros), George Brett (Kansas City Royals), Roberto Clemente (Pittsburgh Pirates), Tony Gwynn (San Diego Padres), Al Kaline (Detroit Tigers), Stan Musial (St. Louis Cardinals), Cal Ripken, Jr. (Baltimore Orioles), Carl Yastrzemski (Boston Red Sox), and Robin Yount (Milwaukee Brewers).

Five Youngest Players to Reach 3,000 Hits

Ty Cobb (34 years, 244 days)
Hank Aaron (36 years, 101 days)
Robin Yount (36 years, 359 days)
Derek Jeter (37 years, 13 days)
Pete Rose (37 years, 21 days)

"I try not to change anything in the postseason. I don't like to say you focus more in the postseason, because that sounds like you're focusing less during the season. But in the postseason you are more focused. You can't help it. Every pitch, every grounder, every inning means more."
—Derek Jeter

Derek is beaming after the Yankees clinch the 2003 American League Division Series. He's played in the postseason every year except two, and holds the post-season career records for games played, at bats, hits, and runs scored.

Inning Eight

CAPTAIN MARVEL

In the gloaming of his career, Jeter struggles to come to terms with the perception that his skills are declining and the skepticism of once-adoring fans, who witness the inevitable erosion of athleticism caused by advancing age. For how long can he defy the odds?

"You're a person a lot longer before and after you're a professional athlete," says Derek. "Your image isn't your character. Character is what you are as a person. That's what I worry about."

Though critics using advanced metrics to evaluate performance continue to label Derek a defensive liability, he wins five Gold Glove Awards during his career. No computer code can measure a player's dedication. "Stats, stats, stats," says Derek. "You can't quantify everything a player does to win games."

Derek's reliable business partner.

A calf injury forces the indomitable Derek to the disabled list during the 2011 season. It is just his fifth career stint on the 15-day inactive list, and his first since 2003. Here he is rehabbing with the Trenton Thunder, the Yankees' Double-A minor league team, on June 13, 2011.

"I'm not only a friend of his, I'm a big fan of his. I just like watching him accomplish all of the things he's accomplished over the years. It's been amazing."
—Tino Martinez

Taking swings off a tee in the batting cage as former teammate Tino Martinez, right, watches.

"There may be people that have more talent than you, but there's no excuse for anyone to work harder than you do."
—Derek Jeter

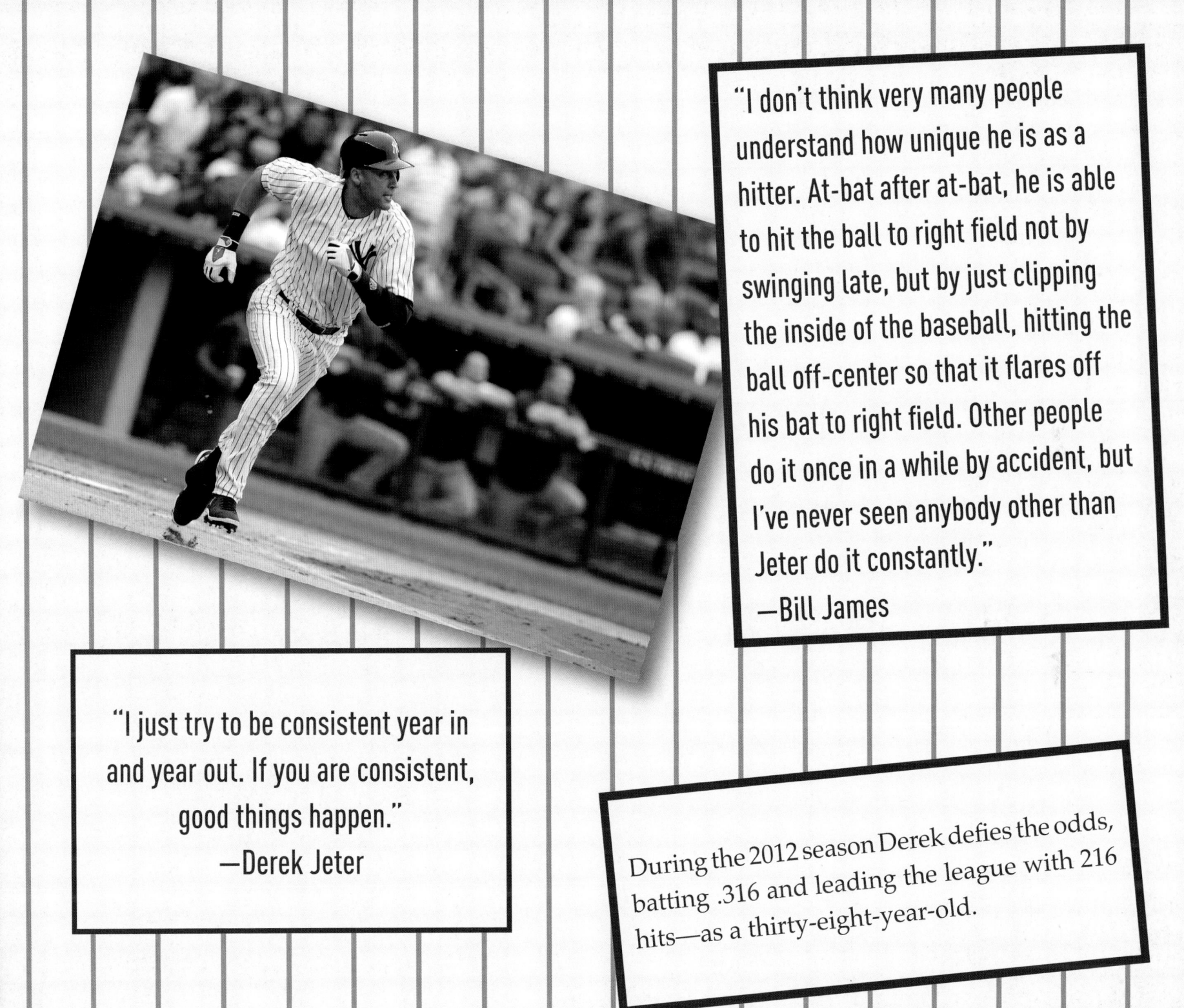

"I don't think very many people understand how unique he is as a hitter. At-bat after at-bat, he is able to hit the ball to right field not by swinging late, but by just clipping the inside of the baseball, hitting the ball off-center so that it flares off his bat to right field. Other people do it once in a while by accident, but I've never seen anybody other than Jeter do it constantly."
—Bill James

"I just try to be consistent year in and year out. If you are consistent, good things happen."
—Derek Jeter

During the 2012 season Derek defies the odds, batting .316 and leading the league with 216 hits—as a thirty-eight-year-old.

"[Jeter] just has to wait for his body to let him know."
—Omar Vizquel, the oldest player ever to play shortstop in the Major Leagues.

Derek lies injured with a fractured left ankle after extending to field a grounder in the 12th inning of Game 1 of the 2012 American League Championship Series. Without their captain to lead them, the Yankees will fall to Detroit in four straight games.

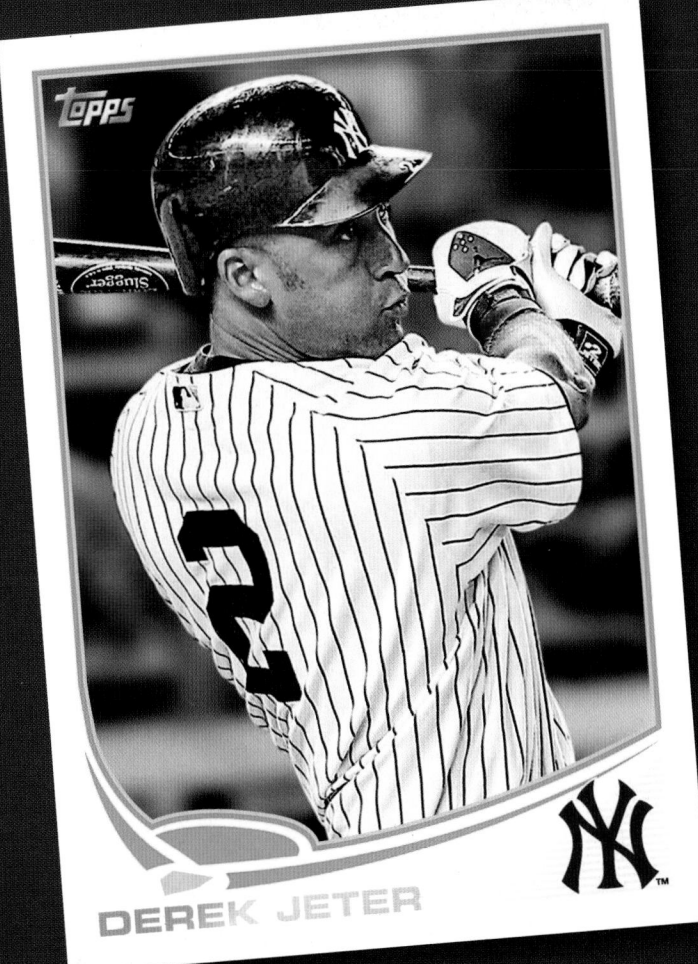

DEREK JETER

Following through on his 2013 Topps baseball card. Playing in only 17 games, Derek has only 63 at-bats and hits .190, more than 120 points below his career average.

"Knowing the type of care he's gotten, I think he's going to come back very strong. He's going to shut a lot of people up. I think you're going to see a resiliency here that this person's always had. To have that type of success in professional sports requires unbelievable focus and dedication."

—Dr. Rock Positano, New York's Hospital for Special Surgery, before Derek Jeter's final season

Inning Nine

COOPERSTOWN CALLING

Five years after his retirement, Jeter is a certain lock for unanimous induction into the Hall of Fame. This chapter reviews all the trophies, accolades, and achievements.

Derek was just twenty-eight-years old when he was named captain in 2003, but he has earned the respect of his peers. He is the longest-serving Yankee captain, with 2014 marking his twelfth season in the role.

"Whenever there's a problem in the clubhouse—there are a lot of little problems on the Yankees— Derek is the first one to step in and say, 'What's the problem? We've got to cut this out.' I really looked up to him. Playing in New York is a pressure job. It's hard being the captain of the Yankees. But he has never stumbled."
—Chris Hammond, former teammate

"This is a great honor. Captain of the Yankees is not a title that is thrown around lightly. It is a huge responsibility and one that I take very seriously. I thank Mr. Steinbrenner for having such confidence in me."
—Derek Jeter

Derek is all smiles at the news conference announcing he is the winner of the American League Rookie of the Year award, receiving all 28 first-place votes awarded. He is the eighth Yankee to win the award, but the first since Dave Righetti in 1981.

"We had a lot of guys who were valuable. I don't think we had one guy, player-wise, who was more valuable than him."
—Joe Torre

Derek takes home the 2000 All-Star Game Most Valuable Player Award. He goes 3-for-3 with a pair of RBIs and a run scored to help the American League to a 6–3 win over the National League at Atlanta's Turner Field.

Derek embraces manager Joe Torre during the World Series trophy presentation, on October 27, 2000. Following his All-Star Game MVP performance, Derek one-upped himself by winning the World Series MVP. In the process he becomes the first to win both MVP awards in the same season.

"The bigger the situation, the more the game speeds up. That's all mental. It messes people up. You think, 'I've got to do this, I've got to do that' when in reality, all you have to do is the same thing you've always been doing. Slow it down. Realize you've been in this situation before. You've been successful in this situation before. Be calm. The more you can do that, the more pressure you take off yourself and the easier it is to perform."
—Derek Jeter

Derek's All-Star Game homer takes flight in 2001. He hits .440 (11-for-25) in All-Star Games.

"The guy's incredible. It doesn't matter if you bat him first or second, that guy's going to hack it. I don't think there's any doubt. He's the leader of this team."
—Yankee reliever Mike Stanton, after Derek is awarded the 2000 World Series MVP

"You can throw him inside as much as you want and he can still fist the ball off. You can throw the ball low and away, and he can hit with power the other way. We have pitchers' meetings, and he's one of those guys where you just stay on the subject for a while. What do you do?"
—Jesse Orosco

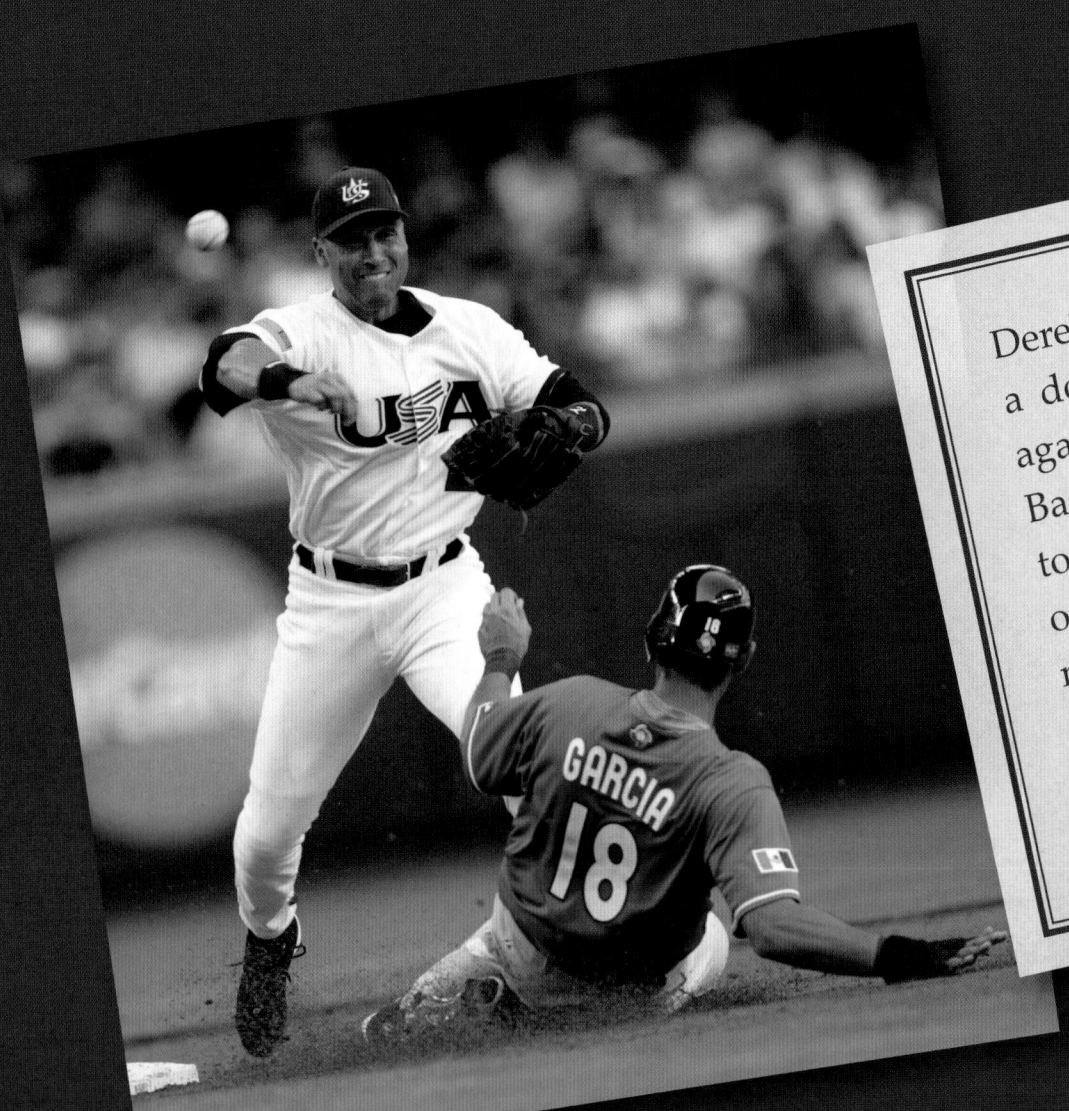

Derek throws to first base to complete a double play in a first-round game against Mexico in the first-ever World Baseball Classic. Played in March prior to the 2006 regular season, Derek is one of the leading hitters in the tournament, batting .450 (9-for-20). He is the captain of Team USA in 2009 when the team reaches the semifinals of the international tournament.

"I had the privilege to call Derek a teammate during the World Baseball Classic and got to see firsthand how to lead by example. I've always been a big Derek Jeter fan for what he has done on the baseball field. I became an even bigger fan after getting to know Derek and learning there is more to this game than what goes on between the lines."
—David Wright

SPORTSMAN of the YEAR

DOUBLE ISSUE

Sports Illustrated

SI.COM

Yankees
Shortstop
**DEREK
JETER**

161 Street–
Yankee Stadium
Station

B D 4

161 St & River Av NE

The 2009 *Sports Illustrated* issue honoring Derek as the magazine's Sportsman of the Year.

"Derek Jeter sets the bar for everyone who puts on a uniform. . . . He's the consummate professional. He plays the game the way it's supposed to be played. And he does it every day. That's why he is the captain of the Yankees."
—Dave Roberts

"When you think about being a good sportsman, there's a lot of things that come to mind. People tell you it's success on the baseball field, and I think that's part of it. I also think there's a lot of qualities that go into it—hard work, dedication, pride, humility. These are all things that I learned at a very young age."
—Derek Jeter

Derek at a news conference at the Yankees spring training complex in Tampa, Florida, on February 19, 2014, announcing he will retire at the end of the season. Derek is a 13-time All-Star with five Gold Glove Awards. He has played in over 2,600 regular season games, only one of which came when his team was mathematically eliminated from the postseason.

"The one thing I always said to myself was that when baseball started to feel more like a job, it would be time to move forward."
—Derek Jeter

"I'm so happy that Derek will get to go out on his terms—and his way. He was as special a teammate as any player could ever have. I'm blessed to have played with him."
—Bernie Williams

"If there's one guy that the game of baseball will miss once he's retired, it's Derek. . . . He is one of the baseball players that pretty much his whole career has done everything perfectly right. And when I watch him play I get goose bumps. You know what I'm saying? That's one of the players that everybody wants to come and see. . . . That's a player that definitely we're all gonna miss after he's done with baseball."
—David Ortiz

"I want to be remembered as someone who had a lot of respect for the game, his teammates, and opponents, and I want to be remembered as a winner. But most importantly, I want to be remembered as a Yankee."
—Derek Jeter

"Derek Jeter has been a great representative of what the Yankees have stood for over the years. He has been a team player who has only cared about winning. He has also been a fine example both on and off the field over his long tenure as a Yankee. It has been a real pleasure to manage him and play alongside him." —Joe Girardi

Extra Innings

DEREK JETER

BY THE NUMBERS—AND BEYOND

From his first major league hit to his career batting record against the best pitchers of his era, Jeter has been the model of consistency and production. He does not merely compile numbers; he contributes to his team winning ball games, both with his otherworldly playing talents and his keen leadership skills. Here we use a rearview mirror to put some career accomplishments in perspective.

Derek Jeter's Hits Milestones

Hit	Date	Opp	Pitcher
1	5/30/95	@SEA	Tim Belcher
1,000	9/25/00	DET	Steve Sparks
1,500	8/17/03	@BAL	Pat Hentgen
2,000	5/26/06	KC	Scott Elarton
2,500	8/22/08	@BAL	Radhames Liz
2,675	8/16/09	@SEA	Doug Fister*
2,721	9/09/09	TB	Chris Richard**
2,722	9/11/09	BAL	Chris Tillman***
3,000	7/09/11	TB	David Price

*Broke Luis Aparicio's record for the most hits by a shortstop.

**Tied Lou Gehrig for all-time Yankees hits record.

***Passed Gehrig to become the Yankees all-time hits leader.

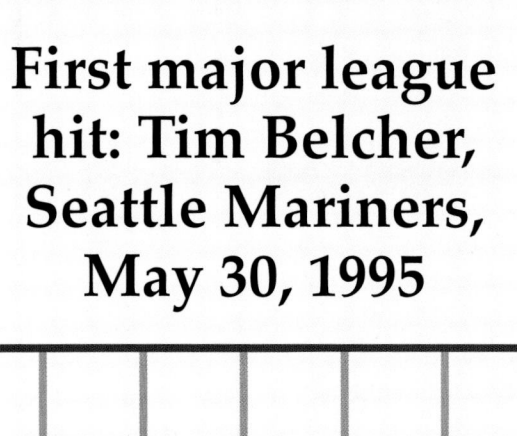

First major league hit: Tim Belcher, Seattle Mariners, May 30, 1995

"People for years to come are going to talk about Derek Jeter's career, and when they look at his bio and see who gave up his first hit, my name will always be there. That's kind of a neat association."

—Tim Belcher

Derek Jeter facing Tim Belcher (regular season career)

25 at bats, 9 hits, 1 double, 2 runs batted in, 3 walks, 4 strikeouts, .360 batting average, .448 on-base percentage, .400 slugging percentage

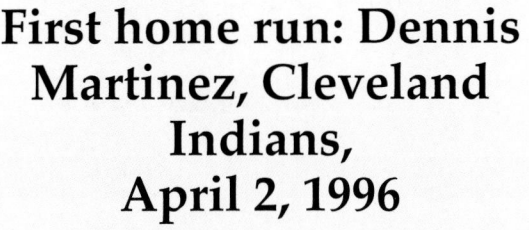

First home run: Dennis Martinez, Cleveland Indians, April 2, 1996

"First time I saw Derek it was a highlight of his first major-league home run. The reason why I remember this so well is because he connected off my former teammate Dennis Martinez. Speaking to Dennis at the end of last season, he was very proud to have given up Derek's initial homer. As for Derek, he connected off a brand name. There is only one El Presidente."
—Ken Singleton

Derek Jeter facing Dennis Martinez (regular season career)

10 at bats, 4 hits, 1 home run, 3 runs batted in, 2 strikeouts, .400 batting average, .455 on-base percentage, .700 slugging percentage

Most at-bats: Tim Wakefield, 125
Most hits: Tim Wakefield, 36

Derek Jeter facing Tim Wakefield (regular season career)

125 at bats, 36 hits, 4 doubles, 1 triple, 3 home runs, 12 runs batted in, 7 walks, 18 strikeouts, .288 batting average, .323 on-base percentage, .408 slugging percentage

"I know I've faced him a lot, and I know he's got a lot of at-bats against me, and he's a great hitter, obviously. For him to be the all-time hit leader in Yankee history is special. It tells you a lot about the kind of player he is. But I think the kind of person he is shows more about him than anything else."
—Tim Wakefield

Highest batting average (minimum 25 plate appearances):
Hideo Nomo, .600 (12-for-20, 5 walks)

Derek Jeter facing Hideo Nomo
(regular season career)

20 at bats, 12 hits, 2 doubles, 1 triple, 5 runs batted in, 5 walks, .600 batting average, .680 on-base percentage, .800 slugging percentage

Most walks: Pedro Martinez, 12

Most strikeouts: Pedro Martinez, 29

Facing Pedro Martinez in the postseason

Here is a review of Jeter's career postseason highlights against Pedro Martinez:

1999 American League Championship Series (Yankees win 4 games to 1)
   In Game 3, Martinez struck out 12 Yankees in seven scoreless innings and allowed just two hits, one by Jeter. It was the Red Sox's lone victory of the series.

2003 American League Championship Series (Yankees win 4 games to 3)

In Game 3, Jeter went 2-for-3 with a home run to help tag Martinez with a loss.

In Game 7, which was the game many felt Boston manager Grady Little stayed with Martinez too long, Pedro retired Jeter the first three times at bat, but allowed a double to the shortstop in the 8th inning when the Yankees rallied to tie the game.

2004 American League Championship Series (Yankees lose 4 games to 3)

In Game 2, the Yankees defeated Martinez, 3–1. Jeter walked, stole second, and scored in the first inning.

In Game 5, Jeter belted a three-run double in the 6th inning to give the Yankees the lead, but the Red Sox came back and won the game in 14 innings.

2009 World Series (Yankees win 4 games to 2)

In Game 2, Pedro, pitching for the Philadelphia Phillies, gave up all three runs in a 3–1 loss. Jeter went 1-for-3 with two strikeouts and a double.

In Game 6, Pedro allowed four runs in four innings—Jeter went 1-for-2 off him.

Derek Jeter facing Pedro Martinez (regular season career)
107 at bats, 29 hits, 6 doubles, 4 home runs, 10 runs batted in, 12 walks, 29 strikeouts, .271 batting average, .350 on-base percentage, .439 slugging percentage

"Depending on the situation, the one [hitter] I did not want to see forever in the postseason was actually Jeter. Jeter was just uncomfortable to pitch to, especially in the postseason. It seems like he won't swing and miss at a pitch. And then you make a great pitch, a quality pitch, and he fouls it off."
— Pedro Martinez

The Best Against the Best

Over the course of his magnificent career, Derek Jeter faced pitchers destined for the Hall of Fame, as well as Cy Young award recipients and winners of over 200 career games. Some hurlers remained fierce rivals, while others became teammates. Here is a recap of Derek's performance against the best pitchers of his era.

Rocket Fuel

Intimidation was a big part of Roger Clemens' success as a power pitcher. Prior to Clemens being traded to the Yankees, he was an ace with the Boston Red Sox and Toronto Blue Jays. Clemens often threw inside pitches to Jeter and drilled him on two occasions, though many more pitches just barely missed the shortstop. "I used to hate facing Roger," Jeter has said. "I thought he might hit me."

When Clemens joined the Yankees for spring training in 1999, Jeter came up with an idea to break the ice between him and his new teammate. Jeter borrowed shin guards, a chest protector, and facemask from catcher Jorge Posada, turned around his own batting helmet, and stepped into the batting cage to face Clemens while wearing a full set of catcher's gear! "He is an intimidating pitcher," says Jeter. "If he is on the other team you don't like facing him."

Derek Jeter facing Roger Clemens (regular season career)

32 at bats, 6 hits, 3 doubles, 1 run batted in, 1 walk, 10 strikeouts, .188 batting average, .235 on-base percentage, .281 slugging percentage

Derek Jeter facing Tom Glavine (regular season career)

35 at bats, 11 hits, 1 double, 3 home runs, 6 runs batted in, 2 walks, 5 strikeouts, .306 batting average, .342 on-base percentage, .583 slugging percentage

Derek Jeter facing Roy Halladay (regular season career)
94 at bats, 22 hits, 4 doubles, 5 runs batted in, 8 walks, 24 strikeouts, .234 batting average, .294 on-base percentage, .277 slugging percentage

"He's nasty. His ball moves. . . . He's not fun to face. He throws hard, it moves, plus he's got that good curveball."
—Derek Jeter on Roy Halladay

Derek Jeter facing Orel Hershiser (regular season career)
21 at bats, 8 hits, 3 doubles, 1 run batted in, 1 walk, 3 strikeouts, .381 batting average, .409 on-base percentage, .524 slugging percentage

"Derek is a leader and veteran presence. His leadership, his advice, his approach at the plate rubs off on the other Yankees. . . . Derek Jeter, I'm a big fan. He's going to lead by example [and] he's going to get his hits."

—Orel Hershiser

Derek Jeter facing Randy Johnson (regular season career)
17 at bats, 3 hits, 1 double, 1 home run, 2 runs batted in, 6 strikeouts, .176 batting average, .176 on-base percentage, .412 slugging percentage

Derek Jeter facing Greg Maddux (regular season career)
26 at bats, 12 hits, 4 runs batted in, 1 walk, 4 strikeouts, .462 batting average, .500 on-base percentage, .462 slugging percentage

"He never throws a ball over the plate, but he hits his spots. He's had a lot of success doing that over the years. . . . He's a great pitcher. That's the best way to put it. Whether you're throwing 95 [mph] or 65 [mph], there's still an art to hitting your spots, and he's mastered it as good as anyone."

—Derek Jeter on Jamie Moyer

Derek Jeter facing Jamie Moyer (regular season career)
74 at bats, 23 hits, 3 doubles, 2 home runs, 3 runs batted in, 5 walks, 3 strikeouts, .311 batting average, .354 on-base percentage, .432 slugging percentage

Derek Jeter facing Mike Mussina (regular season career)

37 at bats, 13 hits, 3 doubles, 1 triple, 1 home run, 5 runs batted in, 1 walk, 6 strikeouts, .351 batting average, .368 on-base percentage, .568 slugging percentage

"We can put on the uniform, and we can play in the Stadium, but we're not the New York Yankees unless Derek Jeter is playing shortstop."
—Mike Mussina

Derek Jeter facing CC Sabathia (regular season career)

29 at bats, 13 hits, 3 doubles, 2 runs batted in, 2 walks, 4 strikeouts, .448 batting average, .484 on-base percentage, .552 slugging percentage

"I'm saddened that he is not going to be around. You want a guy like that to play forever. I'm just happy I got the chance to play with him."
—CC Sabathia

Derek Jeter facing Johan Santana (regular season career)

46 at bats, 19 hits, 5 doubles, 1 home run, 5 runs batted in, 3 walks, 8 strikeouts, .413 batting average, .449 on-base percentage, .587 slugging percentage

Derek Jeter facing Curt Schilling (regular season career)
68 at bats, 20 hits, 1 double, 2 home runs, 8 runs batted in, 2 walks, 13 strikeouts, .294 batting average, .324 on-base percentage, .397 slugging percentage

"He's shown up, played, and turned in a first-ballot Hall of Fame career in the hardest environment in sports. . . . I know competing against that guy, for the decade or so we matched up, was what made the major leagues the major leagues for someone like me."
—Curt Schilling

Derek Jeter facing John Smoltz
(regular season career)
18 at bats, 2 hits, 1 double, 1 walk,
4 strikeouts, .111 batting average,
.158 on-base percentage, .167 slugging percentage

"He believes in what he can do and he's
not resting on his laurels. . . . He's not only
chasing down the people in front of him for the
hits list, but he's playing at a high level. He's a
superstar that has stayed a superstar as long
as I can remember. . . . Age is just a number
for certain guys, and I would say that applies
to Derek Jeter."
—John Smoltz

Future Captain Shows His Stripes

Derek Jeter was named the Yankees captain in 2003, but five years earlier, in 1998, when Jeter was just twenty-four years old, he was already proving himself to be a team leader who would police the clubhouse and his teammates. The Yankees would win 125 games that season. As was his habit in late September once the team had clinched a postseason berth, manager Joe Torre allowed his starters to rest. In one game against the Baltimore Orioles, Torre removed two of his regular outfielders and replaced them with substitute outfielders off the bench. When a blooper fell between the outfielders for a cheap base hit, the pitcher on the mound, David Wells, threw up his hands in frustration and disgust. Jeter noticed the unsportsmanlike display from Wells and later spoke to the pitcher, eleven years his senior, to tell Wells that the Yankees don't behave that way towards their teammates. Wells apologized, and Jeter's teammates were impressed that a young player would naturally take charge of such a situation. Says Torre about Jeter: "We knew from the start that there was something special about him. The way he carried himself, the way he played the game. He's just all about winning."

Derek Jeter facing David Wells (regular season career)
67 at bats, 21 hits, 2 doubles, 4 home runs, 10 runs batted in, 1 walk, 10 strikeouts, .313 batting average, .324 on-base percentage, .522 slugging percentage

"He was a gamer. A big-game hitter, big-game player. Every time we needed a hit, he got one, especially in the playoffs. He killed us in '96 when I was with Baltimore. It was like, 'Are you kidding me? How do you get this guy out?' He was like a gnat—but a Hall of Fame gnat."
—David Wells

References

BOOKS

Allen, Maury. *Yankees World Series Memories*. Sports Publishing L.L.C.; Champaign, Illinois, 2008.

O'Connor, Ian. *The Captain: The Journey of Derek Jeter*. Houghton Mifflin Harcourt, New York, 2011.

One Hundred Years: New York Yankees. The Official Retrospective. New York. Ballantine Books, 2003.

Pietrusza, David; Silverman, Matthew; and Gershman, Michael (eds.). *Baseball: The Biographical Encyclopedia*. New York: Total Sports, 2000.

Stout, Glen. *Yankees Century: 100 Years of New York Yankees Baseball*. Boston: Houghton Mifflin Company, 2002.

PERIODICALS AND WEBSITES

2014 Yankees Media Guide

New York Daily News

The New York Times

Sports Illustrated

www.baseball-almanac.com

www.baseball-reference.com

www.baseballhalloffame.org

www.espn.com

www.newrepublic.com

www.newyork.yankees.mlb.com

www.sportingnews.com

www.turn2foundation.org

Image Credits

Page iii: AP Photo / Ed Reinke

Page 9: AP Photo/Bill Kostroun

Page 10: [left] Topps Baseball Card / Author's Colletion [right] Dave Winfield poster / Author's Collection

Page 11: *Kalamazoo Gazette*/Landov

Page 12: Courtesy of Jeff Idelson/National Baseball Hall of Fame

Page 13: [left] Topps Baseball Card/Author's Collection   [right] AP Photo/Richard Harbus

Page 14: *Yankees Magazine*/Author's Collection

Page 15: [left] AP Photo/Mark Lennihan [right] Ken Babbitt/Four Seam Images

Page 16: AP Photo/Gary Stewart

Page 17: Ticket Stub/Author's Collection

Page 21: AP Photo/Kevork Djansezian

Page 22: AP Photo/Mark Lennihan

Page 23: AP Photo/Mark Lennihan

Page 24: AP Photo/Ron Frehm

Page 25: National Baseball Hall of Fame

Page 29: [left] AP Photo/Osamu Honda [right] AP Photo/Doug Mills

Page 30: AP Photo/Mark J. Terrill

Page 31: [left] AP Photo/Eric Draper [right] AP Photo/ Mark Lennihan

Page 32: National Baseball Hall of Fame

Page 33: AP Photo/Amy Sancetta [right] AP Photo/Marty Lederhandler

Page 34: AP Photo/Bill Kostroun

Page 35: AP Photo/Mark Lennihan

Page 36: AP Photo/Amy Sancetta

Page 37: *Sports Illustrated* Magazine/Author's Collection

Page 41: AP Photo/Bill Kostroun

Page 42: AP Photo/Charles Krupa

Page 43: AP Photo/Jae C. Hong

Page 44: AP Photo/Bill Kostroun

Page 45: *GQ* Magazine/Author's Collection

Page 46: AP Photo/Julie Jacobson

Page 47: AP Photo/Gene J. Puskar

Page 48: Wikimedia Commons/Photojunkie

Page 49: AP Photo/Gail Burton

Page 50: AP Photo/Tony Gutierrez

Page 51: AP Photo/Kathy Willens

Page 55: AP Photo/Eric Risberg

Page 56: AP Photo/Ben Margot

Page 57: AP Photo/Amy Sancetta

Page 58: [left and right] AP Photo/Bill Kostroun

Page 59: [left] AP Photo/Kathy Willens [right] AP Photo/Rusty Kennedy

Page 60: AP Photo/Charles Krupa